MW01110432

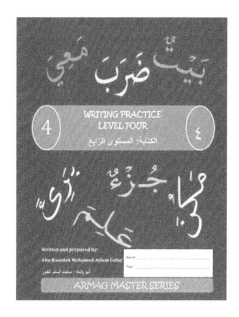

Mohamed Aslam Gafur

Mobile: +44 7468574251

e-mail: aslamgafur@yahoo.co.uk

Published and distributed by

AMAZON.COM

AMAZON.CA

AMAZON.UK

AMAZON.EU

Website:

www.amazon.co.uk/s?k=aslam+gafur&ref=nb_sb_noss_2

FAST TRACK:

Type my name, **"Aslam Gafur"** in Amazon search bar for all titles.

CONTENT

Lesson one: Arabic writing practice
Second Grade Extension:
Alif

حرف الألف

أ أ أ أ أ

Skills are graded according to the accuracy of writing the letter properly and on the lines.

a) Write the letter Alif (أ ﺄ ﺄ) on the lines provided.

Start here ⟵

Joining	End	Middle	Beginning	By itself
أ أ أ	ﺄ	ﺄ	أ	أ

			أَصُلَ

			بَأَرَ

			خَبَأً

c) Write the words on the lines provided. **Start here** ←

			أَصُلَ

			بَأَرَ

			خَبَأً

Teacher's comment: تعليق المدرّس/ المدرّسة

Lesson two: Arabic writing practice

Second Grade Extension:

Baa

حرف الباء

Skills are graded according to the accuracy of writing the letter properly and on the lines.

a) Write the letter Baa (ب ـب ـبـ) on the lines provided.

Start here ←

End	Middle	Beginning	By itself
ـب	ـبـ	بـ	ب

Page | 6

b) Write the letter Baa (‫ب ـب ـب‬) on the lines provided.

			بـ بـ ب
			بـ بـ ب
			بـ بـ ب
			بـ بـ ب

c) Write the letter Baa (‫بـب‬) on the lines provided.

			بيب
			بيب
			بيب
			بيب

			بَشَرَ
			هَبَطَ
			قَلَب

			بَشَرَ
			هَبَطَ
			قَلَب

Teacher's comment: تعليق المدرّس/ المدرّسة

Open Taa

حرف التّاء المفتوحة

ت ـتـ ـت

Skills are graded according to the accuracy of writing the letter properly and on the lines.

a) Write the Open Taa (ت ـتـ ـت) on the lines provided.   **Start here** ←

End	Middle	Beginning	By itself
ـت	ـتـ	تـ	ت

b) Write the Open Taa (ﺗ ﺘ ﺖ) on the lines provided.

			تـتـت
			تـتـت
			تـتـت
			تـتـت

c) Write the Open Taa (تت) on the lines provided.

			تت
			تت
			تت
			تت

d) Write the words on the lines provided. **Start here**

			تَفِهَ
			خَتَمَ
			بُهِتَ

e) Write the words on the lines provided. **Start here**

			تَفِهَ
			خَتَمَ
			بُهِتَ

Teacher's comment: تعليق المدرّس/ المدرّسة

Second Grade Extension: Round Taa

حرف التّاء المربوطة

ة ـة

Skills are graded according to the accuracy of writing the letter properly and on the lines.

a) Write the Round Taa (ة ـة) on the lines provided.   **Start here** ←

			ة
			ة
			ة
			ـة
			ـة
			ـة
			ـة

b) Write the words on the lines provided.

			بَقَرَةٌ
			هُمَزَةٌ
			حَسَنَةٌ
			جَمِيلَةٌ
			بَقَرَةٌ
			هُمَزَةٌ
			حَسَنَةٌ
			جَمِيلَةٌ

Teacher's comment: تعليق المدرّس/ المدرّسة

Skills are graded according to the accuracy of writing the letter properly and on the lines.

a) Write the letter Thaa (ثـ ـثـ ـث) on the lines provided.   **Start here** ←

End	Middle	Beginning	By itself
ـث	ـثـ	ثـ	ث

b) Write the letter Thaa (ثـ ـثـ ـث) on the lines provided.

			ثـثـث
			ثـثـث
			ثـثـث
			ثـثـث

c) Write the letter Thaa (ـثـثـ) on the lines provided.

			ثثـ
			ثثـ
			ثثـ
			ثثـ

d) Write the words on the lines provided.

			ثَلَمَ

			نُشِرَ

			بَحَثَ

e) Write the words on the lines provided.

			ثلَمَ

			نُشِرَ

			بَحَثَ

Teacher's comment: تعليق المدرّس/ المدرّسة

Lesson six: Arabic writing practice
Second Grade Extension:

Jeem

حرف الجيم

Skills are graded according to the accuracy of writing the letter properly and on the lines.

a) Write the letter Jeem (جـ ← ـجـ ← ـج) on the lines provided.

Start here ←

End	Middle	Beginning	By itself
ـج	ـجـ	جـ	ج

b) Write the letter Jeem (ج ـج ـجـ) on the lines provided.

			جـ ـجـ ـج
			جـ ـجـ ـج
			جـ ـجـ ـج
			جـ ـجـ ـج

c) Write the letter Jeem (جـج) on the lines provided.

			جـجـج
			جـجـج
			جـجـج
			جـجـج

d) Write the words on the lines provided. Start here ←

			جَعَلَ
			سُجِدَ
			نَتَجَ

e) Write the words on the lines provided. Start here ←

			جَعَلَ
			سُجِدَ
			نَتَجَ

Teacher's comment: تعليق المدرّس/ المدرّسة

Lesson seven: Arabic writing practice

Second Grade Extension:

Haa

حرف الحاء

ح ـح ـحـ حـ

Skills are graded according to the accuracy of writing the letter properly and on the lines.

a) Write the letter Haa (ح ـحـ ـح ح) on the lines provided.

Start here ←

End	Middle	Beginning	By itself
ح	حـ	ـح	ح

b) Write the letter Haa (‎ح ‎ـح ‎ـحـ) on the lines provided.

			‎ح ‎ـحـ ‎حـ
			‎ح ‎ـحـ ‎حـ
			‎ح ‎ـحـ ‎حـ
			‎ح ‎ـحـ ‎حـ

c) Write the letter Haa (‎حـح ‎ـح) on the lines provided.

			‎حح ‎ـح
			‎حح ‎ـح
			‎حح ‎ـح
			‎حح ‎ـح

			حَـمَـلَ

			نَـحَـرَ

			فُـتِـحَ

d) Write the words on the lines provided.   Start here ←

			حَمَلَ

			نَحَرَ

			فُتِحَ

Teacher's comment: تعليق المدرّس/ المدرّسة

Lesson eight: Arabic writing practice
Second Grade Extension:
Khaa

حرف الخاء

خـ ـخـ ـخ

Skills are graded according to the accuracy of writing the letter properly and on the lines.

a) Write the letter Khaa (خ ـخـ ـخ) on the lines provided.

Start here ←

End	Middle	Beginning	By itself
خ	ـخـ	خـ	خ

b) Write the letter Khaa (خ ـخ ـخ) on the lines provided.

			خ ـخ ـخ
			خ ـخ ـخ
			خ ـخ ـخ
			خ ـخ ـخ

c) Write the letter Khaa (خـخـخ) on the lines provided.

			خـخـخ
			خـخـخ
			خـخـخ
			خـخـخ

d) Write the words on the lines provided.

			خَـلَـقَ

			سَـخِـرَ

			نُـفِـخَ

e) Write the words on the lines provided.

			خَلَقَ

			سَخِرَ

			نُفِخَ

Teacher's comment: تعليق المدرّس/ المدرّسة

Lesson nine: Arabic writing practice

Second Grade Extension:

Daal

Skills are graded according to the accuracy of writing the letter properly and on the lines.

حرف الدّال
د د د

a) **Write the letter Daal (د ـد ـد) on the lines provided.**   **Start here** ←

End	Middle	Beginning	By itself
ـد	ـد	د	د

			ﺪ ﻟ ﻟ
			ﺪ ﻟ ﻟ
			ﺪ ﻟ ﻟ
			ﺪ ﻟ ﻟ

c) Write the letter Daal (ﺪ ﺪ ﺪ) on the lines provided.

			ﺩ ﺩ ﺩ
			ﺩ ﺩ ﺩ
			ﺩ ﺩ ﺩ
			ﺩ ﺩ ﺩ

d) Write the words on the lines provided.

			دَخَلَ
			مَدَحَ
			فَسَدَ

e) Write the words on the lines provided.

			دَخَلَ
			مَدَحَ
			فَسَدَ

Teacher's comment: تعليق المدرّس/ المدرّسة

Lesson ten: Arabic writing practice

Second Grade Extension:

Dhaal

حرف الذّال

ذ ذ ذ

Skills are graded according to the accuracy of writing the letter properly and on the lines.

a) Write the letter Dhaal (ذ ذ ذ) on the lines provided.

Start here ←

End	Middle	Beginning	By itself
ذ	ذ	ذ	ذ

b) Write the letter Dhaal (ذ ذ ذ) on the lines provided.

			ذ ـذ ذ
			ذ ـذ ذ
			ذ ـذ ذ
			ذ ـذ ذ

c) Write the letter Dhaal (ذ ذ ذ) on the lines provided.

			ذ ذ ذ
			ذ ذ ذ
			ذ ذ ذ
			ذ ذ ذ

d) Write the words on the lines provided.

			ذَعِنَ

			كَذِب

			نَفَذَ

e) Write the words on the lines provided.

			ذَعِنَ

			كَذِبَ

			نَفَذَ

Teacher's comment: تعليق المدرّس/ المدرّسة

Lesson eleven: Arabic writing practice

Second Grade Extension:

Raa

حرف الرّاء

ر ر ر

Skills are graded according to the accuracy of writing the letter properly and on the lines.

a) Write the letter Raa (ر ر ر) on the lines provided.

Start here ⬅

End	Middle	Beginning	By itself
ر	ر	ر	ر

ﺭ ﺭ ﺭ

ﺭ ﺭ ﺭ

ﺭ ﺭ ﺭ

ﺭ ﺭ ﺭ

c) Write the letter Raa (ﺭ ﺭ ﺭ) on the lines provided.

ﺭ ﺭ ﺭ

ﺭ ﺭ ﺭ

ﺭ ﺭ ﺭ

ﺭ ﺭ ﺭ

d) Write the words on the lines provided.

			رَ مَ قَ
			شَ رِ بَ
			نُ صِ رَ

e) Write the words on the lines provided.

			رَمَقَ
			شَرِبَ
			نُصِرَ

Teacher's comment: تعليق المدرّس/ المدرّسة

Second Grade Extension:

Zaay

حرف الزّاي

ز ـزـ ـز

Skills are graded according to the accuracy of writing the letter properly and on the lines.

a) Write the letter Zaay (ز ـزـ ـز) on the lines provided.

Start here ←

End	Middle	Beginning	By itself
ـز	ـزـ	ز	ز

b) Write the letter Zaay (ـز ـزـ) on the lines provided.

			ز ـزـ ـز
			ز ـزـ ـز
			ز ـزـ ـز
			ز ـزـ ـز

c) Write the letter Zaay (ز ز ز) on the lines provided.

			ز ز ز
			ر ر ر
			ر ر ر
			ر ر ر

d) Write the words on the lines provided. **Start here** ←

			زَعَمَ
			خَزَلَ
			لَمَزَ

e) Write the words on the lines provided. **Start here** ←

			زَعَمَ
			خَزَلَ
			لَمَزَ

Teacher's comment: تعليق المدرّس/ المدرّسة

Semester one test: **Date:**......./......./.............

Name of student:...   **Age:**.................................

a) Circle the following letters (11 marks)

Raa	Baa	Khaa	Alif	Dhaal	Haa
ر - د	ب - ث	خ - خ	ل - ا	ز - ذ	ح - ج

Jeem	Taa	Zaay	Daal	Thaa
خ - ج	ث - ت	ذ - ز	د - ر	ت - ث

b) Write the following letters on the line provided. (12 marks)

أ أ أ أ	ذ ذ ذ ذ	ج ج ج	ب ب ب

c) Write the following words on the line provided (12 marks)

سِنَةٌ	خَزَلَ	سُجِدَ	أَسِفَ

d) Use a ruler and draw a straight line to match the correct letters. (5 marks)

جنة	ب
ترك	ج
بصل	ث
حكم	ت
ثلج	ح

Class participation:......................./ 30	**General behaviour**...................../ 30
Test:................................./ 40	**TOTAL MARKS:**........................./ 100

This is to certify that

_____

has successfully completed the School's programme
of training and passed the first semester examination on

ARABIC WRITING

in testimony whereof we have awarded this

Level 1 Second Grade Certificate

with the grade of

_____

On ..../......../..................

Principal   Teacher

....

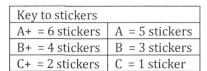

Key to stickers	
A+ = 6 stickers	A = 5 stickers
B+ = 4 stickers	B = 3 stickers
C+ = 2 stickers	C = 1 sticker

Lesson thirteen: Arabic writing practice
Second Grade Extension: Seen

حرف السّين

س ـسـ ـس

Skills are graded according to the accuracy of writing the letter properly and on the lines.

a) Write the letter Seen (س ـس ـسـ ـس) on the lines provided. **Start here** ←

End	Middle	Beginning	By itself
ـس	ـسـ	سـ	س

b) Write the letter Seen (س ـس ـسـ) on the lines provided.

			سـ ـسـ ـس
			سـ ـسـ ـس
			سـ ـسـ ـس
			سـ ـسـ ـس

c) Write the letter Seen (سسس) on the lines provided.

			سسسس
			سسسس
			سسسس
			سسسس

Start here

d) Write the words on the lines provided.

			سَـلَـكَ

			نَـسِـيَ

			عَـبَـسَ

Start here

e) Write the words on the lines provided.

			سَلَكَ

			نَسِيَ

			عَبَسَ

Teacher's comment: تعليق المدرّس/ المدرّسة

Lesson fourteen: Arabic writing practice
Second Grade Extension:

Sheen

حرف الشّين

شـ ـشـ ش

Skills are graded according to the accuracy of writing the letter properly and on the lines.

a) Write the letter Sheen (ش ـشـ ـش ش) on the lines provided. **Start here** ←

End	Middle	Beginning	By itself
ـش	ـشـ	شـ	ش

b) Write the letter Sheen (شـ ـشـ ـش) on the lines provided.

			شـ ـشـ ـش
			شـ ـشـ ـش
			شـ ـشـ ـش
			شـ ـشـ ـش

c) Write the letter Sheen (ـشـش) on the lines provided.

			شـشـش
			شـشـش
			شـشـش
			شـشـش

d) Write the words on the lines provided.

			شَكَرَ
			خَشِيَ
			كَبَشَ

e) Write the words on the lines provided.

			شَكَرَ
			خَشِيَ
			كَبَشَ

Teacher's comment: تعليق المدرّس/ المدرّسة

Skills are graded according to the accuracy of writing the letter properly and on the lines.

a) Write the letter Saad (ص ـص ـص ص) on the lines provided.   Start here ←

End	Middle	Beginning	By itself
ـص	ـصـ	صـ	ص

b) Write the letter Saad (ص ـصـ ـص) on the lines provided.

			صـ ـصـ ـص
			صـ ـصـ ـص
			صـ ـصـ ـص
			صـ ـصـ ـص

c) Write the letter Saad (صـص) on the lines provided.

			صـصـص
			صـصـص
			صـصـص
			صـصـص

d) Write the words on the lines provided.

			صَـلَـحَ
			بُـصِـمَ
			نَـقَـصَ

e) Write the words on the lines provided.

			صَلَحَ
			بُصِمَ
			نَقَصَ

Teacher's comment: تعليق المدرّس/ المدرّسة

Lesson sixteen: Arabic writing practice
Second Grade Extension:
Daad

حرف الضّاد

ض ـض ـضـ

Skills are graded according to the accuracy of writing the letter properly and on the lines.

a) Write the letter Daad (ض ـضـ ـض) on the lines provided. **Start here** ←

End	Middle	Beginning	By itself
ـض	ـضـ	ضـ	ض

b) Write the letter Daad (ض ضـ ـضـ) on the lines provided.

			ضـ ـضـ ض
			ضـ ـضـ ض
			ضـ ـضـ ض
			ضـ ـضـ ض

c) Write the letter Daad (ـضـ ض) on the lines provided.

			ضـضـض
			ضـضـض
			ضـضـض
			ضـضـض

			ضَـمُـرَ
			قُـضِـيَ
			رَ فَـضَ

			ضَمُرَ
			قُضِيَ
			رَفَضَ

Teacher's comment: تعليق المدرّس/ المدرّسة

Lesson seventeen: Arabic writing practice
Second Grade Extension:
Taa

حرف الطّاء

ط ط ط

Skills are graded according to the accuracy of writing the letter properly and on the lines.

a) Write the letter Taa (ط ط ط) on the lines provided.   **Start here** ←

End	Middle	Beginning	By itself
ط	ط	ط	ط

			ط ط ط
			ط ط ط
			ط ط ط
			ط ط ط

c) Write the letter Taa (ططط) on the lines provided.

			ططط
			ططط
			ططط
			ططط

			طَلَعَ
			خَطَبَ
			غَلِطَ

			طَلَعَ
			خَطَبَ
			غَلِطَ

Teacher's comment: تعليق المدرّس/ المدرّسة

Lesson eighteen: Arabic writing practice
Second Grade Extension:
Dhaa

حرف الظّاء

ظ ظ ظ

Skills are graded according to the accuracy of writing the letter properly and on the lines.

a) Write the letter Dhaa (ظ ظ ظ) on the lines provided.

Start here

End	Middle	Beginning	By itself
ظ	ظ	ظ	ظ

b) Write the letter Dhaa (ظ ظ ظ) on the lines provided.

			ظ ظ ظ
			ظ ظ ظ
			ظ ظ ظ
			ظ ظ ظ

c) Write the letter Dhaa (ظظظ) on the lines provided.

			ظظظ
			ظظظ
			ظظظ
			ظظظ

d) Write the words on the lines provided.

			ظَـهَـرَ
			عَـظُـمَ
			حَـفِـظَ

e) Write the words on the lines provided.

			ظَهَرَ
			عَظُمَ
			حَفِظَ

Teacher's comment: تعليق المدرّس/ المدرّسة

Lesson nineteen: Arabic writing practice
Second Grade Extension: 'Ayn

Skills are graded according to the accuracy of writing the letter properly and on the lines.

a) Write the letter 'Ayn (ع ــع ــعــ ع) on the lines provided.  **Start here**

End	Middle	Beginning	By itself
ع	ــعــ	عـ	ع

b) Write the letter 'Ayn (ع ـعـ ـع) on the lines provided.

			ع ع ع
			ع ع ع
			ع ع ع
			ع ع ع

c) Write the letter 'Ayn (عع) on the lines provided.

			عع
			عع
			عع
			عع

			عَلِمَ

			فُعِلَ

			جَمَعَ

			عَلِمَ

			فُعِلَ

			جَمَعَ

Teacher's comment: تعليق المدرّس/ المدرّسة

Lesson twenty: Arabic writing practice

Second Grade Extension:

Ghyn

حرف الغين

غ ـغـ ـغ

Skills are graded according to the accuracy of writing the letter properly and on the lines.

a) Write the letter Ghyn (غ ـغـ ـغ) on the lines provided.

Start here ⟵

End	Middle	Beginning	By itself
ـغ	ـغـ	غـ	غ

b) Write the letter Ghyn (غ ـغـ غ) on the lines provided.

			غ ـغـ غ
			غ ـغـ غ
			غ ـغـ غ
			غ ـغـ غ

c) Write the letter Ghyn (ـغـ عـ) on the lines provided.

			غغغ
			غغغ
			غغغ
			غغغ

Start here

d) Write the words on the lines provided.

			غَسَـلَ
			نَغِـلَ
			بَـلَـغَ

Start here

e) Write the words on the lines provided.

			غَسَـلَ
			نَغِلَ
			بَلَغَ

Teacher's comment: تعليق المدرّس/ المدرّسة

Lesson twenty-one: Arabic writing practice
Second Grade Extension:
Faa

Skills are graded according to the accuracy of writing the letter properly and on the lines.

a) Write the letter Faa (ف ـف ـفـ فـ) on the lines provided.   Start here ◄——

End	Middle	Beginning	By itself
ـف	ـفـ	فـ	ف

b) Write the letter Faa (ﻑ ـﻓ ـﻒ) on the lines provided.

			ف ـﻓ ـﻒ
			ف ـﻓ ـﻒ
			ف ـﻓ ـﻒ
			ف ـﻓ ـﻒ

c) Write the letter Faa (ﻓﻔﻒ) on the lines provided.

			ﻓﻔﻒ
			ﻓﻔﻒ
			ﻓﻔﻒ
			ﻓﻔﻒ

d) Write the words on the lines provided.

			فَتَحَ
			نُفِثَ
			كَشَفَ

e) Write the words on the lines provided.

			فَتَحَ
			نُفِثَ
			كَشَفَ

Teacher's comment: تعليق المدرّس/ المدرّسة

Lesson twenty-two: Arabic writing practice

Second Grade Extension: Qaaf

Skills are graded according to the accuracy of writing the letter properly and on the lines.

a) Write the letter Qaaf (ق ـق ـقـ) on the lines provided.

Start here ◀—

End	Middle	Beginning	By itself
ق	ـقـ	قـ	ق

b) Write the letter Qaaf (قَ ـقـ ق) on the lines provided.

			قـقـق
			قـقـق
			قـقـق
			قـقـق

c) Write the letter Qaaf (قفق) on the lines provided.

			ققق
			ققق
			ققق
			ققق

d) Write the words on the lines provided.

			قَـتَـلَ

			ثَـقُـلَ

			خَـلَـقَ

e) Write the words on the lines provided.

			قَتَلَ

			ثَقُلَ

			خَلَقَ

Teacher's comment: تعليق المدرّس/ المدرّسة

Semester two test: Date:......./......./............

Name of student:...   Age:...............................

a) Circle the following letters (11 marks)

Faa	Daad	Seen	Ghyn	Taa	Sheen
غ - ف - غ	ض - ع	س - ظ	غ - ف	ص - ط	ق - ش

Saad	Qaaf	Faa	'Ayn	Dhaa
ص - ع	ط - ق	ف - ش	س - ع	ض - ظ

b) Write the following letters on the line provided. (12 marks)

ق ـ ق ق	ظ ظ ظ	ص ـ ص ص	غ ـ غ ـ غ

c) Write the following words on the line provided (12 marks)

كَبَش	مَسَح	فَـعَـلَ	ظُـلِـمَ

d) Use a ruler and draw a straight line to match the correct letters. (5 marks)

غُلِبَ	ش
صَرَفَ	ط
شَرِبَ	غ
طَلَعَ	ق
قَمَرَ	ص

Class participation:...................../ 30	General behaviour.................../ 30
Test:................................/ 40	TOTAL MARKS:........................./ 100

This is to certify that

_____

has successfully completed the School's programme
of training and passed the first semester examination on

ARABIC WRITING

in testimony whereof we have awarded this

Level 2 Second Grade Certificate

with the grade of

_____

On ..../......../.................

Principal   Teacher

....

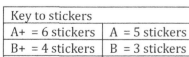

Key to stickers	
A+ = 6 stickers	A = 5 stickers
B+ = 4 stickers	B = 3 stickers
C+ = 2 stickers	C = 1 sticker

Second Grade Extension:

Kaaf

حرف الكاف

ك ك ك

Skills are graded according to the accuracy of writing the letter properly and on the lines.

a) Write the letter Kaaf (ك ك ك) on the lines provided.

Start here ←

End	Middle	Beginning	By itself
ك	ك	ك	ك

b) Write the letter Qaaf (كـ ـكـ ـك) on the lines provided.

			كـ ـكـ ـك
			كـ ـكـ ـك
			كـ ـكـ ـك
			كـ ـكـ ـك

c) Write the letter Qaaf (ككك) on the lines provided.

			ككك
			ككك
			ككك
			ككك

d) Write the words on the lines provided.

Start here ←

			كَشَفَ

			حَكَمَ

			هَلَكَ

e) Write the words on the lines provided.

Start here ←

			كَشَفَ

			حَكَمَ

			هَلَكَ

Teacher's comment: تعليق المدرّس/ المدرّسة

Lesson twenty-four: Arabic writing practice

Second Grade Extension:

Laam

Skills are graded according to the accuracy of writing the letter properly and on the lines.

a) Write the letter Laam (ل ـل ـلـ لـ) on the lines provided.

Start here ←

End	Middle	Beginning	By itself
ـل	ـلـ	لـ	ل

b) Write the letter Laam (‏ل ـل ـلـ‏) on the lines provided.

			‏لـلـل‏
			‏لـلـل‏
			‏لـلـل‏
			‏لـلـل‏

c) Write the letter Laam (‏لـلل‏) on the lines provided.

			‏لل‏
			‏لل‏
			‏لل‏
			‏لل‏

d) Write the words on the lines provided.

			لَفَظَ

			غُلِبَ

			نَكَلَ

e) Write the words on the lines provided.

			لَفَظَ

			غُلِبَ

			نَكَلَ

Teacher's comment: تعليق المدرّس/ المدرّسة

حرف الميم

م ـمـ مـ

Lesson twenty-five: Arabic writing practice

Second Grade Extension:

Meem

Skills are graded according to the accuracy of writing the letter properly and on the lines.

a) Write the letter Meem (م ـمـ مـ) on the lines provided.

Start here ←

End	Middle	Beginning	By itself
ـم	ـمـ	مـ	م

b) Write the letter Meem (مـ ـمـ ـم) on the lines provided.

			مـ ـمـ ـم
			مـ ـمـ ـم
			مـ ـمـ ـم
			مـ ـمـ ـم

c) Write the letter Meem (لـلـل) on the lines provided.

			مـمـم
			مـمـم
			مـمـم
			مـمـم

d) Write the words on the lines provided.

			مَسَـح

			حَمِـدَ

			بُـصِـمَ

e) Write the words on the lines provided.

			مَسَح

			حَمِدَ

			بُصِمَ

Teacher's comment: تعليق المدرّس/ المدرّسة

Lesson twenty-six: Arabic writing practice
Second Grade Extension:
Noon

Skills are graded according to the accuracy of writing the letter properly and on the lines.

حرف النون

ن ـذ ـن

a) Write the letter Noon (ن ـنـ ـن) on the lines provided.

Start here ←

End	Middle	Beginning	By itself
ـن	ـنـ	نـ	ن

b) Write the letter Noon (‫ن ـنـ نـ‬) on the lines provided.

			‫نـنـن‬
			‫نـنـن‬
			‫نـنـن‬
			‫نـنـن‬

c) Write the letter Noon (‫نن‬) on the lines provided.

			‫نن‬
			‫نن‬
			‫نن‬
			‫نن‬

d) Write the words on the lines provided. Start here ←

			نَـجَـرَ
			بُـنِـيَ
			مَـكُـنَ

e) Write the words on the lines provided. Start here ←

			نَجَرَ
			بُنِيَ
			مَكُنَ

Teacher's comment: تعليق المدرّس / المدرّسة

Lesson twenty-seven: Arabic writing practice
Second Grade Extension:

Haa

حرف الهاء

Skills are graded according to the accuracy of writing the letter properly and on the lines.

a) Write the letter Haa (‍ه ‍ه ـه ه / هـ) on the lines provided.

Start here ←

End	Middle	Beginning	By itself
‍ه	‍ه‍	هـ	ه / ه

b) Write the letter Haa (ـه ـهـ هـ) on the lines provided.

			ـه ـهـ هـ
			ـه ـهـ هـ
			ـه ـهـ هـ
			ـه ـهـ هـ

c) Write the letter Haa (ههه) on the lines provided.

			ههه
			ههه
			ههه
			ههه

			هَـمَـلكَ

			نَـهَـرَ

			جَـبَـةَ

			هَمَلكَ

			نَهَرَ

			جَبَةَ

Teacher's comment: تعليق المدرّس/ المدرّسة

Lesson twenty-eight: Arabic writing practice

Second Grade Extension:

Waaw

حرف الواو

Skills are graded according to the accuracy of writing the letter properly and on the lines.

a) Write the letter Waaw (و و) on the lines provided.

Start here ←

End	Middle	Beginning	By itself
ـو	ـو	و	و

b) Write the letter Waaw (و و و) on the lines provided.

			و و و
			و و و
			و و و
			و و و

c) Write the letter Waaw (و و و) on the lines provided.

			و و و
			و و و
			و و و
			و و و

			وُجِدَ

			قَوِيَ

			فَهُوَ

			وُجِدَ

			قَوِيَ

			فَهُوَ

Teacher's comment: تعليق المدرّس/ المدرّسة

Second Grade Extension:

Hamzah

حرف الهمزة

أ ؤ ئ

Skills are graded according to the accuracy of writing the letter properly and on the lines.

a) Write the letter Hamzah (ء أ ؤ ئ) on the lines provided. Start here ←

End	Middle	Beginning	By itself
ئ ؤ إ أ	ؤ ئـ	أ إ	ء

ءَ ا مَ ـنَ	أَ مَ ـرَ	إِ رَ مُ
بَ ـأَ ـرَ	فَ إِ ن	خَ ـطَ ـأَ
بِ ـنَ ـجَ ـإِ	بَ ـؤُ ـسَ	لُؤُ لُؤٌ
بِ ـئْ ـسَ	يَ ـوْ ـمَ ـئِ ـذٍ بَ ـرِ ـئَ	
جَ ا ءَ	شَ ا ءَ قَ ا ءَ	

إِرَمُ	أَمَرَ	عَامَنَ
خَطَأً	فَإِنْ	بَأَرَ
لُؤْلُؤٌ	بَؤُسَ	بِنَبَإٍ
بَرِىءٌ	يَوْمَئِذٍ	بِئْسَ
قَاءَ	شَاءَ	جَاءَ

Teacher's comment: تعليق المدرّس/ المدرّسة

Lesson thirty: Arabic writing practice
Second Grade Extension:
Yaa

Skills are graded according to the accuracy of writing the letter properly and on the lines.

a) Write the letter Yaa (ي ـ ـيـ ـي) on the lines provided.

Start here ←

End	Middle	Beginning	By itself
ي	ـيـ	يـ	ي

b) Write the letter Yaa (ي ـيـ يـ) on the lines provided.

			يـيـي
			يـيـي
			يـيـي
			يـيـي

c) Write the letter Yaa (ـيـبـ) on the lines provided.

			يـيي
			يـيي
			يـيي
			يـيي

			يَلِدُ

			بَيْنَ

			خَشِيَ

			يَلِدُ

			بَيْنَ

			خَشِيَ

Teacher's comment: تعليق المدرّس/ المدرّسة

Semester three test: Date:......./......./..............

Name of student:..   Age:.................................

a) Circle the following letters (11 marks)

Faa	Daad	Seen	Ghyn	Taa	Sheen
ف - غ	ض - ع	س - ظ	غ - ف	ص - ط	ق - ش

Saad	Qaaf	Faa	'Ayn	Dhaa
ص - ع	ط - ق	ف - ش	س - ع	ض - ظ

b) Write the following letters on the line provided. (12 marks)

ق ق ق	ظ ظ ظ	ص ص ص	غ غ غ

c) Write the following words on the line provided (12 marks)

كَبَش	مَسَح	فَعَلَ	ظُلِمَ

d) Use a ruler and draw a straight line to match the correct letters. (5 marks)

غُلِبَ	ش
صَرَفَ	ط
شَرِبَ	غ
طَلَعَ	ق
قَمَرَ	ص

Class participation:...................../ 30	General behaviour...................../ 30
Test:.............................../ 40	TOTAL MARKS:........................./ 100

This is to certify that

_____

has successfully completed the School's programme
of training and passed the first semester examination on

ARABIC WRITING

in testimony whereof we have awarded this

Level 3 Second Grade Certificate

with the grade of

_____

On ……./……./………………

Principal   Teacher

……………………………………   ………………………………………….

Key to stickers	
A+ = 6 stickers	A = 5 stickers
B+ = 4 stickers	B = 3 stickers
C+ = 2 stickers	C = 1 sticker

Made in the USA
Coppell, TX
22 March 2025

47410939R00057